Our Government

The
State Governor

by Mary Firestone

Consultant:
Kathleen Skidmore-Williams
National Governors Association
Washington, D.C.

Capstone press

Mankato, Minnesota

First Facts is published by Capstone Press,
151 Good Counsel Drive, P.O. Box 669, Mankato, Minnesota 56002.
www.capstonepress.com

Library of Congress Cataloging-in-Publication Data
Firestone, Mary.
     The state governor / by Mary Firestone.
     p. cm.—(First facts. Our government)
     Summary: Introduces the executive branch of state government and the role of
the governor.
     Includes bibliographical references and index.
     ISBN 0-7368-2500-2 (hardcover)
     ISBN 0-7368-4692-1 (paperback)
     1. Governors—United States—Juvenile literature. 2. State governments—United States—
Juvenile literature. [1. Governors. 2. State governments.] I. Title. II. Series.
JK2447.F57 2004
352.23′213′0973—dc22   2003013201

Editorial Credits
Christine Peterson, editor; Jennifer Bergstrom, designer; Jo Miller, photo researcher;
     Eric Kudalis, product planning editor

Photo Credits
AP/Wide World Photos/Al Goldis, 17; Carlos Osorio, 13; Don Wright, 14; Governor's Office,
     Michaele White, 8–9; Greg Wahl-Stephens, 18–19; Nathan Martin, 15
Corbis/Paul Barton, 5
Getty Images Inc./Bob Bird, 7; Spencer Platt, 11
The State of New Jersey, cover
Unicorn Stock Photos/Jeffrey Greenberg, 20

1 2 3 4 5 6 09 08 07 06 05 04

Table of Contents

Governors Help Keep Kids Safe

State governors sign new laws to keep kids safe. In Oregon, the governor signed a new law about wearing safety helmets. Kids in that state must wear safety helmets when using inline skates, skateboards, or scooters. State governors work to keep kids safe.

State Government

State government has three parts.
The **legislative** branch writes **bills**. The
judicial branch decides what laws mean.

Parts of State Government

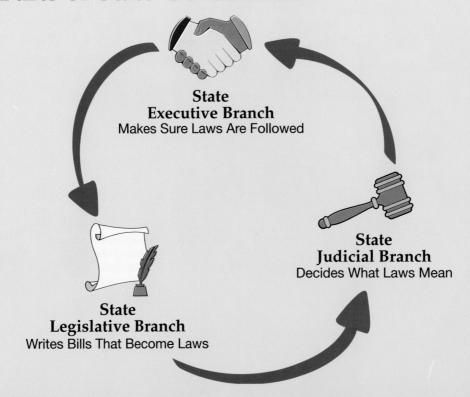

**State
Executive Branch**
Makes Sure Laws Are Followed

**State
Judicial Branch**
Decides What Laws Mean

**State
Legislative Branch**
Writes Bills That Become Laws

The executive branch leads state government. The governor leads this part of state government. This branch makes sure people follow state laws.

Governors Are Leaders

Governors are leaders of their states. They are in charge of their states' **military**. They sign bills into laws or **veto** them. Governors share ideas on how to spend state money. They choose some state leaders.

States Have Rules for Governors

People must follow state rules to become governor. Governors must live in the states they serve. They have to be U.S. **citizens**. They must be at least 25 years old. In some states, governors must be at least 30 years old.

 Fun Fact
Before taking office, many governors served as state lawmakers.

People Elect Governors

People elect governors to lead their states. People vote for **candidates** on election day. Governors promise to make sure people follow state laws. Governors serve **terms** that last two or four years. In most states, governors can serve more than one term.

 Fun Fact

In 13 states, governors can serve any number of terms in a row.

13

Governors Have Busy Days

Governors have busy days filled with meetings. They meet with state lawmakers to decide how to spend money. They also talk about bills.

14

Governors also meet with people in their states. They visit schools to talk with teachers and kids. Governors listen to their ideas.

Governors Work at the Capitol

Most governors work in offices at their state capitols. Governors study bills in their offices. They make phone calls. They read letters. They also talk to state lawmakers.

 Fun Fact

Since 1925, 25 women have served as governor. Three women have served as governor of Arizona.

People Help Governors

Governors choose people to help them. These leaders are in charge of the states' schools, health care, and roads. Lieutenant governors lead most states when governors cannot. They also work on bills with governors and state lawmakers.

19

Amazing But True!

Most governors live in a special house or mansion. Many of these houses were built just for governors and their families. People also can visit the mansions.

The governor's mansion in Maine (pictured above) is located in the capital city of Augusta.

Hands On: Write Your Governor

State governors like to hear what kids think about their state. Write a letter to your governor. Tell the governor what you like about your state. Give the governor ideas for improving your state.

What You Need

an adult to help	envelope
pencil	postage stamp
paper	

What You Do

1. Ask an adult to help you find the address for your governor in the newspaper or library. Addresses for all state governors can also be found at *http://www.nga.org/governors*.
2. Begin your letter with "Dear Governor."
3. Write a letter telling the governor what you like about your state and why. Write down ideas for improving things in your state. Give three reasons why you think your idea would help the state.
4. Sign your letter.
5. Put the letter in an envelope.
6. Place a postage stamp on the envelope's upper right corner.
7. Address the envelope.
8. Ask an adult to help mail the letter.

Glossary

bill (BIL)—a written idea for a new law

candidate (KAN-di-date)—a person who runs for office

citizen (SIT-i-zuhn)—a person who is part of a nation by birth or choice

judicial (joo-DISH-uhl)—the branch of state government includes courts; the judicial branch explains laws.

legislative (LEJ-uh-slay-tiv)—the branch of state government that writes and passes bills that may become laws

military (MIL-uh-ter-ee)—the armed forces of a state or country

term (TERM)—a set period of time that elected leaders serve in office

veto (VEE-toh)—the power or right to stop a bill from becoming law

Read More

Giesecke, Ernestine. *State Government.* Kids' Guide. Chicago: Heinemann Library, 2000.

LeVert, Suzanne. *The Governor.* Kaleidoscope. New York: Benchmark Books, 2004.

Murphy, Patricia J. *Election Day.* Rookie Read-About Holidays. New York: Children's Press, 2002.

Internet Sites

FactHound offers a safe, fun way to find Internet sites related to this book. All of the sites on FactHound have been researched by our staff.

Here's how:
1) Visit *www.facthound.com*
2) Type in this special code **0736825002** for age-appropriate sites. Or enter a search word related to this book for a more general search.
3) Click on the Fetch It button.

FactHound will fetch the best sites for you!

Index